The Dunbar
Martyrs

The cover shows a detail of a portrait of Oliver Cromwell by Peter Lely, and a detail of an engraving of Durham Cathedral by Robert Billings, both reproduced by kind permission of Durham County Council. All pictures in the text marked 'DCC' are likewise printed by kind permission of Durham County Council. Pictures attributed to 'Billings' are from R.W. Billings' *Architectural Illustrations and Description of the Cathedral Church at Durham*, 1843

The Dunbar
Martyrs

Scottish Prisoners of War
in Durham Cathedral, 1650

Simon Webb

Contents

Frontispiece of Hobbes' Leviathan

Whatsoever therefore is consequent to a time of war, where every man is enemy to every man; the same is consequent to the time, wherein men live without other security, than what their own strength, and their own invention shall furnish them withal. In such condition, there is no place for industry; because the fruit thereof is uncertain; and consequently no culture of the earth; no navigation, nor use of the commodities that may be imported by sea; no commodious building; no instruments of moving, and removing such things as require much force; no knowledge of the face of the earth; no account of time; no arts; no letters; no society; and which is worst of all, continual fear, and danger of violent death; and the life of man, solitary, poor, nasty, brutish, and short.

Thomas Hobbes, *Leviathan*, 1651

Dean Barwick, from the frontispiece of his
biography, written by his brother Peter

I. Devastation

In the winter of 1660, John Barwick, the new dean of Durham, visited his cathedral for the first time as dean.

What he saw inside the mighty Norman church must have chilled his heart. The roof leaked, and the northern winds penetrated the broken windows. Many of the ancient monuments of the cathedral were missing, or had been mutilated, including the font: the damage done to the fourteenth-century tombs of Ralph and Alice, and John and Maud Neville can still be seen today.

The stone effigies of Ralph and John, a father and son who were both powerful local magnates of their time, had been reduced to headless, limbless torsos. Their wives, Alice and Maud, were not spared similar treatment: Maud was the only one of the four to have kept her head, but her face was so badly smashed that there were no facial features left.

As is quite common for aristocratic tombs of this period, the stone effigies of the noble quartet lie on elaborately-carved stone boxes. Back in

1660, Dean Barwick would no doubt have been shown how all the heads had been broken off a frieze of small figures that adorns the base of Ralph and Alice's tomb, while the frieze around John and Maud's stone box had been completely stripped away.

Looking around in the nave, Barwick, who had known Durham for nearly twenty years, could not have helped but notice that almost all the familiar woodwork in the cathedral, including the organ-cases, had gone, and that there were scorch-marks on the stone pavement. The only wooden structure still remaining was Prior Castell's clock, an immense time-piece, taller than most people's houses, which still stands proud in its corner of the great church, having survived the Reformation, the civil wars, and two world wars.

If, after his first tour of the cathedral as dean, John Barwick left by the ornate north door, he could have walked right over the grimmest reminder of the dark times that Durham had seen a decade before: the unmarked mass graves of hundreds of Scottish men and boys.

It is possible to trace the origins of the tragic events that unfolded in and around Durham Cathedral from 1650 to something that took place during the afternoon of the thirtieth of January in the preceding year – 1649. It was then that King Charles I stepped out of a window onto a high scaffold that had been erected in front of the magnificent Banqueting House in Whitehall, built during the reign of Charles's father, King James I. Minutes after he stepped onto the scaffold, Charles I was beheaded by a masked, anonymous executioner. At that moment, an immense moan issued from the huge crowd that had assembled to watch the decapitation of the king. According to one observer, it was a sound such 'as I never heard before and desire I may never hear again'. After the execution, the royal head was held up to show the people, though the headsman broke with tradition and did not cry out, 'This is the head of a traitor', probably fearing that somebody present would recognise his voice. Many people in the crowd then pressed forward to dip their handkerchiefs in the king's blood, to keep as souvenirs.

Given that he was publicly murdered by his own people, it seems hardly necessary to write that Charles I was an unpopular and an unlucky king. One reason for his unpopularity was his stance on religion.

In order to understand the bloodthirsty politics of the time it is necessary to grasp the fact that in the seventeenth century in Britain, and indeed in much of Europe, politics and religion were bound together in a suffocating embrace. On the Protestant side, religious and political thinking were characterised by a rabid fear and hatred of the Roman Catholic religion, its supporters and its priests. The pope was regularly referred to as the Antichrist, and even in the more relaxed atmosphere of the reign of Charles II, disasters such as the Great Fire of London were routinely blamed on the Catholics: until 1830 the Monument to the Great Fire ended its description of the Fire itself with the words 'But Popish frenzy, which wrought such horrors, is not yet quenched'.

The Protestant Puritans who came to dominate British politics in the seventeenth century were uneasy about Charles I's queen, the diminutive French Catholic princess, Henrietta Maria. Might she not attempt to bring up her children in the Catholic faith; might she not be plotting with Catholics on the Continent to overthrow British Protestantism and, worse, might she not be trying to sway her royal husband toward the religion of Rome?

Charles's own version of Protestantism seemed too Roman Catholic for many of his Puritan subjects, especially in Scotland where Protestant opinion was very much in favour of plain speaking, plain churches, and priests in plain outfits leading very plain services. Many of the Puritans in both England and Scotland wanted to render the organisation of their national churches more plain by removing some elements that appeared too Roman. In particular, many favoured the Presbyterian form of church organisation, which has no bishops or archbishops.

At an important conference at Hampton Court in 1604, Charles's father James I had rejected Presbyterianism in no uncertain terms, on the basis that it was inconsistent with the monarchy. 'No bishop, no King', James had snapped. 'When I mean to live under a presbytery I will go to Scotland again'. James was of course the monarch who had started off as king of Scotland, but became king of England as well on the death of the childless queen Elizabeth I.

It is likely that most people in twenty-first century Britain do not think about bishops from one year's end to the next: by contrast, in the seventeenth century, bishops became an obsession for many people, who viewed them either as a symptom of the kind of church and state they did not want, or a characteristic of what they *did* want. In his satirical poem *Hudibras*, the first part of which was published in 1663, Samuel Butler poured scorn on the enthusiasms of the middle of the century, describing how:

> The oyster-women lock'd their fish up,
> And trudg'd away, to cry, *no Bishop*.

The question of bishops: whether they should exist at all, or whether their power and wealth should be curtailed, was bound to have a special significance in Durham, where the bishops had had a unique set of powers for centuries. Durham was the 'land of the prince bishops', known simply as 'Bishoprick' to many, where the bishop ruled like a king between the Tyne and the Tees.

When it came to 'Presbytery', Charles I agreed with his father: he wanted bishops and archbishops; but he also wanted to see more elaborate services, buildings and vestments in the national church, together with more sophisticated use of music. In this he was backed by the aforementioned John Barwick, later the dean of Durham; John Cosin, later its bishop, and William Laud, Charles's archbishop of Canterbury from 1633.

The attempt to introduce the elaborate new 'Laudian' style of liturgy caused consternation in England. When John Cosin, who was then a prebendary at Durham cathedral, tried to reform the liturgy of the great church in this direction in the 1620s, he was criticised for introducing music from 'organs, sackbuts and cornets'; for using a cope with an embroidered picture of the Trinity on it, and complaining rudely when some women in the congregation failed to stand up at the appropriate time during a service: 'Can ye not stand, ye lazy sows?' Cosin is alleged to have asked them. (A sackbut is an early type of trombone.)

If the new liturgy caused consternation in England, the first attempt to introduce it into what is now called St Giles' Cathedral in Edinburgh, where Presbyterianism had found a home among the Scottish Protestants, led to a riot. On the twenty-third of July 1637, the brave attempt was made. According to William Maitland, an eighteenth-century historian of Edinburgh:

No sooner had James Hannay, Dean of Edinburgh, appeared in his surplice, and began to read the service, than a number of women, with clapping of hands, execrations, and hideous exclamations, raised a great confusion in the church, which Dr. Lindsay Bishop of Edinburgh willing to appease, stepped into the pulpit, and reminded people of the sanctity of the place: but this, instead of calming, enraged them to such a degree that Janet Geddes, a furious woman, ushered in the dreadful and destructive civil war, by throwing a stool at the bishop's head: and had it not been for the magistrates of Edinburgh, who turned out the frantic multitude, they would probably have murdered him; but such was the noise without, by knocking at the doors, throwing stones in at the windows, and incessant cries of Pape, Pape, Antichrist, pull him down, that the said magistrates were obliged to go out to appease their fury. But the populace watching his return homewards, renewed the assault, that, had he not been rescued by a superior force, they would undoubtedly have dispatched him. Thus began those horrible troubles, which ended in the destruction of the King, subversion of the Church and State, and loss of the rights and liberties of the people.

Concerned that there might be further attempts to enforce the new liturgy on the Scots, Archibald Johnston, Lord Warriston, of whom more later, revived the old idea of a written covenant that Scots could sign, committing themselves to the preservation of their distinctive form of Christianity, while at the same time professing loyalty to the king. Among other things, the signatories of 1638 promised not 'to approve the ecclesiastical government by bishops, nor to their seat and voice in the parliament and courts of justice, until a free meeting of an assembly and parliament had decided these matters'.

This was the beginning of the seventeenth-century Scottish Covenanter movement, which had an immense effect on the subsequent history of Scotland, England, continental Europe and the New World. As the passage from Maitland's 1753 *History of Edinburgh* printed above would seem to suggest, the Covenanters became part of the explosive religious and political mix that ignited at the time of the civil wars. Janet or 'Jenny' Geddes, who threw the stool at the bishop, was supposed to have been a local market-trader; perhaps a less specialised version of Samuel Butler's 'oyster-women' who trudged off to cry, 'No bishop'. It is possible that Jenny never actually existed, but her stool-throwing continues to be recounted in histories of Scotland.

Charles II, engraving of a portrait
by Adrian Hanneman

II. The Battle of Dunbar

As soon as the blade of the axe hit the block at Whitehall in 1649, Charles II became king of England and Scotland. At the time, he was barely out of his teens, and in exile with his mother on the Continent, and the kingdom he was supposed to inherit had been declared a commonwealth or republic. The act that established the new republic stated that England 'shall from henceforth be governed as a commonwealth and free state . . . without any king or House of Lords'. This meant that the young Charles's status was then like that of those interesting people who are still to be met with in various parts of the world, who would be kings, queens, emperors or empresses if their countries had not become republics years ago. A current example would be the ninety-four year old Prince Andrew Romanov, who would be Tsar of Russia if things had not fallen out as they did during the twentieth century.

As the gangly, dark-haired second Charles was

growing up, his father had no doubt expected that he would inherit his kingdom and his fortune. In the event, Charles II inherited little more than the remains of the complex political and religious chess-game that his father had been playing against his enemies for years.

The first Charles had played so badly that his son found few useful pieces on his side of the board in that winter of 1649. One of the few pieces that seemed to offer any promise was Scotland. The Stuart dynasty, to which Charles belonged, was of course Scottish in origin, and soon Edinburgh was planning to use the exiled young king as, in effect, a stick with which to beat the English – or at least, that is how it looked from the English perspective.

At Breda, a city in the southern Netherlands, Charles signed the Treaty of Breda in May 1650. He agreed to accompany the representatives of the Scottish parliament back to Scotland, and, crucially, to sign one of those celebrated Scottish covenants, the Solemn League and Covenant of 1643.

The 1643 covenant went further than the one that had been so widely subscribed to by Scots in 1638. The 1638 signatories had promised not to approve 'ecclesiastical government by bishops' until this vexed question had been put to a 'free meeting of an assembly and parliament'. The signatories of the new Covenant of 1643 promised 'the extirpation' of 'popery, prelacy (that is, Church government by archbishops, bishops, their chancellors and commissaries, deans, deans and chapters, and other ecclesiastical officers depending on that hierarchy)'. Note that 'popery' and 'prelacy' are only separated by a comma here, implying perhaps that they are practically the same.

The Solemn League and Covenant had been widely signed outside of Scotland, for instance by the English, whom the Scots insisted should subscribe as a condition of their joining the English parliament's civil war against King Charles I. The new Covenant had clauses that applied directly to England: signatories promised to *preserve* 'the reformed religion of the Church of Scotland' but to *reform* 'religion in the kingdoms of England and Ireland' to promote 'the nearest conjunction and uniformity in religion' between the three kingdoms, so that 'the Lord may delight to live in the midst of us'.

Although the Lord may have delighted to live in the midst of the people of three reformed united kingdoms where Presbyterianism on the Scottish model held sway, in 1650 it was clear that the exiled Charles II would not have delighted to live in, or to rule, any such kingdoms if there were to be no bishops or archbishops in them. With hindsight, we can remember that, the year after he had been restored to his kingdoms in 1660, Charles II approved the 1661 Sedition Act, which made the Solemn League and Covenant unlawful. As for 'popery', the second Charles had already spent time in France trying to marry a wealthy Catholic heiress; he later married a Portuguese Catholic princess, Catherine of Braganza, passed his crown on to his Catholic brother, James II, and himself converted to Roman Catholicism on his death-bed in 1685.

The Scots insisted that Charles sign the 1643 Covenant, and also the earlier 1638 Covenant, because at the time their parliament was dominated by Presbyterians, the so-called 'Kirk Party'. Once the young king had signed, the Scots promised to restore him to his Scottish throne, although both sides knew perfectly well that Charles could never be wholeheartedly committed to Presbyterianism, and was really not the kind of young man the Scottish Puritans approved of. By 1650 he had already fathered an illegitimate son by his Welsh mistress, Lucy Walter, and he would later acknowledge a number of other illegitimate children.

The Kirk Party were also unhappy about Charles's parentage, and in August 1650 he felt obliged to sign the so-called Dunfermline Declaration, re-affirming his commitment to the Covenants, and also expressing his sense of shame about some of the behaviour of his father (who had only died eighteen months earlier) and the 'idolatry' of his Roman Catholic mother (who was still alive at the time). He also had to admit to his own 'sinfulness'.

As soon as the English parliament got wind of Charles's presence in Scotland, they began the prepare an army to meet any royalist invasion of England that the Scots might be planning: it was assumed that the Scots would use Charles as an excuse to invade. The command of this army was given to one of the most effective parliamentary generals of the recent civil wars: Thomas, Lord Fairfax, the victor of the Battle of Naseby in Northamptonshire in 1645. Fairfax's deputy or Lieutenant-General was to be Oliver Cromwell. But when preparation for a possible Scottish invasion turned into a plan to invade Scotland, in what we would now call a pre-emptive strike, 'Black Tom' backed out. His decision to do so might have had something to do with his wife, the formidable Anne, who was herself a Presbyterian.

With Fairfax out of the picture, Cromwell became Lord General of the campaign to invade Scotland, and on the twenty-second of July 1650 he crossed the border at Berwick with over sixteen thousand men at his back. On his way north, he had stopped at Durham, and is supposed to have stayed overnight in a building that is now part of the Royal County Hotel on Old Elvet. Certainly there is a fine seventeenth-century staircase there, complete with acanthus-leaf carvings, but it is thought to date from around 1660; in other words two years after Cromwell's death, and ten years after his 1650 visit to Durham. The stair-case also started its life in a castle in Scotland, so that although visitors to Durham are regularly told that Cromwell stayed at the Royal County, the idea of him going up to bed via this staircase is pure fantasy. It is also unlikely that any of the old buildings that were combined into the hotel were actually standing in 1650.

At Durham, wherever he stayed, Cromwell was feasted by Sir Arthur Hesilrige, who was then governor of Newcastle and a powerful man throughout the north-east, including in County Durham, where the traditional power of the Prince Bishop did not exist at this time. Also at Durham, Oliver noticed that there were several fine buildings that had once been used by the bishop and the dean and chapter of the cathedral, that were now empty and falling into disrepair. He proposed starting a new college in these buildings, and the plan progressed a little, but died with Cromwell himself: Durham had to wait until 1832 to get its own university, which now occupies several buildings that once belonged to the church.

Cromwell's plan of campaign against the Scots was to march west along the top of what we might call the eastern shoulder of Scotland via the port of Dunbar to Edinburgh, keeping the North Sea and then the Firth of Forth to his right. The English army would capture places like Dunbar, Haddington and Musselburgh *en route* to the Scottish capital, and would be supplied by sea.

It is about sixty miles from Berwick to Edinburgh, Dunbar lying roughly half-way along the route. Because of regular attacks from the Scots, Cromwell found himself repeatedly falling back to Musselburgh, about six miles to the east of the Scottish capital. When the English army finally got a good look at Edinburgh, they found that Oliver's counterpart on the Scottish side, the wily old Alexander Leslie, Earl of Leven, had fortified the city with earthworks, batteries and entrenchments so extensive that nobody had ever seen the like in Britain during the whole of the civil wars. Despite repeated efforts, the English could make little impression on these defences, and the Scots were too wise to come out and fight at a time that was convenient to the invaders.

And Cromwell now had other problems. The wet, cold, stormy weather meant that he was not being as well-supplied by sea as he had hoped, and there was little for his soldiers to eat in the surrounding countryside. It seems that the local Scots had responded to the news of an English invasion by following some advice on the future conduct of Scottish wars supposedly offered by Robert the Bruce on his death-bed in 1329. This included a suggestion about how the Scots should prepare the ground for an enemy army:

> . . . burn the plain land them before:
> Then shall they pass away in haste,

As well as burning their crops as they fled before the advancing army, the Scots took all their four-legged animals with them, so that fresh local mutton, lamb, beef and milk were off the menu for the stricken Roundheads. When, by chance, some of Cromwell's soldiers found a churn of good Scottish cream, they greedily scooped it up and drank it from their helmets: Oliver's surprisingly good sense of humour was tickled when the one soldier without a helmet tried to drink straight from the churn, covered himself with cream, then got the churn stuck on his head.

Cromwell's men were facing starvation, cold and wet, and it is not surprising that many grew sick, the 'flux' being a symptom that Oliver mentioned in dispatches. The 'flux' meant diarrhoea, in this case probably a symptom of dysentery, a frequent visitor to the civil war armies, especially when they had inadequate quarters and were forced to stay in the field too long. The situation was made worse by the fact that in 1650 Europe was at the lowest point in what is now known as the 'Little Ice Age', an unusually cold period with entirely natural causes, which led to poor harvests and the famous London frost fairs, when the Thames froze over and something like a temporary village could be built on it.

After forty days in Scotland, the cold, discouraged, sick, hungry and harassed English army retreated to Dunbar on the first of September, and soon found themselves boxed in by a large Scottish army led by General David Leslie. Trapped between the sea and Leslie's force, which may have comprised as many as fourteen thousand men, the English, who had now been reduced by disease and death to perhaps eleven thousand, could do little at first except gaze up at the Scots' commanding position on Doon Hill.

The situation seemed desperate: Cromwell's route via the village of Cockburnspath to Berwick was blocked, and the future Lord Protector was seen riding around on a small Scotch pony, biting his lip until the blood ran down his chin, but apparently not even noticing that he was bleeding at all.

He wrote a panicky letter to the aforementioned Sir Arthur Hesilrige, addressed to him 'at Newcastle or elsewhere . . . haste, haste':

The enemy hath blocked-up our way at the pass at Copperspath [sic], through which we cannot get without almost a miracle. He lieth so much upon the hills that we know not how to come that way without great difficulty; and our lying here daily consumeth our men, who fall sick beyond imagination . . . indeed, do you get together what forces you can against them. Send to friends in the south to help with more . . .

What happened next was the Battle of Dunbar, which started before dawn on the third of September 1650. Although everybody knows *when* and *where* the battle happened, the *why* and the *how* are still a matter of dispute. English and Scottish sources and commentators interpret the bloody events of the day quite differently.

According to Cromwell and others on the English side, the Scots' general David Leslie foolishly ordered some of his men to descend from their commanding position on Doon Hill, so that they would be in a better position to attack. This was on the second of September, the day when Cromwell wrote his panicky letter to Hesilrige. Cromwell and his officers immediately spotted that this was a mistake, and that Leslie had actually put his men into a position where the English could attack them more easily. Cromwell praised God for delivering the Scots into his hands so unexpectedly, and a successful English attack was launched very early the next morning.

English accounts put much of the blame for the Scottish defeat on the leading members of the pious Kirk Party who were attached to their army, who insisted on having their say in military decisions. These included the aforementioned Johnston of Warriston, the pious Edinburgh lawyer who was co-architect of the seventeenth-century Scottish Covenanter movement. Warriston and his associates are charged with purging the Scottish army of many officers whom they considered to be insufficiently pious, but who were talented and experienced soldiers who would have fought bravely for their king and country. The Kirk men are also supposed to have persuaded David Leslie to move those men down the hill and into harm's way.

According to the Scottish historian Stuart Reid's 2004 book on the campaign, the Scots had to get off the top of Doon Hill because they were too exposed to the dreadful weather up there, and many of them were already sick. By moving closer to the English, they were also better able to prevent their enemies from escaping. According to Reid, Cromwell's early morning attack started as a desperate bid to break out, but when the English officers saw that it was going well, they decided to turn the action into an attempt to rout the whole of Leslie's army.

Also according to Reid, the attempts by Warriston and others to purge the Scottish army were minor affairs, and the Earl of Leven managed to turn them to his own advantage. Reid implies that the Kirk Party should not be blamed for Leslie's supposedly disastrous move down the hill, because it was a wise move in any case.

Both Reid's account and various English versions, old and new, agree that many of the Scottish officers had deserted their men on the night of the second of September to go off and sleep somewhere other than on a cold, wet hillside, under a hay-rick. The leader of the Scottish army, the Earl of Leven, was not there either, but since he was seventy years old at the time he can hardly be blamed for staying in Edinburgh, the city he had fortified so well.

Both sides also acknowledge that many of the Scots had been ordered to extinguish the fuses on their muskets on the night before the battle. These were matchlock muskets, of the type that worked by pressing a smouldering slow fuse into a pan of gunpowder, which, with luck, then ignited and set off the powder in the barrel, firing out a lead ball. If they were faulty, or being used by unskilled musketeers, such weapons could produce the proverbial 'flash in the pan' that did not ignite the powder inside. Without a lighted fuse, no gunpowder could ignite at all, as many of the Scots learned to their cost at the Battle of Dunbar. The wet conditions at Dunbar in September 1650 may also have caused some of the fuses to go out of themselves, or cool to the point where they could not ignite gunpowder in any case.

Unable to reply to enemy fire, the Scots musketeers were terribly vulnerable, and many were mown down by Cromwell's famous 'Ironsides', heavy cavalry on enormous horses. Although many put up a brave fight with pikes, musket-butts, swords, firelock muskets and, when they could get them working, matchlock muskets, in less than an hour the Scots were scattered and running for their lives. Cromwell's cavalry chased them for about eight miles, hunting them and cutting them down.

'Jockie', a typical Scottish soldier of the period, based on a contemporary print (Patricia Brown)

View of the nave of Durham Cathedral, showing damage to the Neville Tombs (Billings, DCC)

Prior Castell's clock (Billings, DCC)

The Battle of Naseby, engraving by J. Sturt, 1702
(DCC)

III. A Day-bed for the Devil

Some of the Scottish refugees from the battle had the good luck to bump into a lady called Anne Murray, who was then travelling through the country. Anne had been a maid employed by Charles II's mother, and she set up an impromptu hospital for the wounded men and boys who stumbled into her path. The patients of this early Scottish version of Mary Seacole or Florence Nightingale included a man with a head-injury, and a boy in his teens who had a wound from a sword.

When victory seemed to have been secured, Cromwell was visited by a prolonged bout of hysterical laughter: this seems to have been too long and intense to be anything to do with his sense of humour. It was more likely a macabre psychological reaction, a release of the extreme tension that had caused him to bite deeply into his own bottom lip in the hours before the battle.

Oliver reckoned that three thousand Scots had

been killed at Dunbar, but very few of his own men. Estimates vary wildly, but the English may have taken around six thousand prisoners, of whom about a thousand were released straight away because they were judged to be too sick or wounded to be any further threat to the English. Perhaps five thousand prisoners began a forced march south into England. This was when the story of the Dunbar martyrs really began.

At first, the prisoners were entrusted to four troops of Colonel Francis Hacker's cavalry, who were to escort them south as far as Berwick. When they reached Newcastle, they would come under the control of the aforementioned governor of that city, Sir Arthur Hesilrige. In a letter dated from Dunbar on the fifth of September, Cromwell told Hesilrige that:

We can find no way how to dispose of these prisoners that will be consisting with these two ends (to wit, the not loosing them, and the not starving them, neither of which would we willingly incur) but by sending them into England.

This implies that Cromwell already had enough trouble feeding and caring for his own soldiers, and wanted to get what he called the 'five thousand poor wretches' of Scottish soldiers off his hands as soon as possible. He proposed that the Council of State for Scottish and Irish Affairs down in London should decide what to do with them, in such a way that 'they may not suddenly return to your prejudice'; in other words, take up arms against England again. Later, on the ninth of September, Cromwell wrote to Hesilrige that:

I hope your northern guests are come to you by this time, I pray you let humanity be exercised towards them, I am persuaded it will be comely. Let the officers be kept at Newcastle some, some sent to Lynn, some to Chester.

Whether he was really concerned for their well-being or not, Cromwell's order to transfer the prisoners out of their own country was against the etiquette of war at the time, and would certainly contravene the modern Geneva Conventions.

In both of his letters to Hesilrige Cromwell mentioned the prisoners, but also included urgent requests for the governor of Newcastle to supply him with horses, men and provisions from his north of England bailiwick as soon as possible, as his own men continued to be in a very poor state. The English had been low on provisions for some time, and they were now probably coming to the end of the supplies they had seized from the defeated Scots. And Cromwell knew that he would soon have to return to Edinburgh to make the most of his victory at Dunbar, and seize control of as much of Scotland as possible: this would require fresh men, horses and provisions.

In his letter of the fifth, Cromwell remarked that transporting the prisoners would not be 'every day's work', even for a 'man of business' like Hesilrige; and certainly the business of transporting five thousand starving, exhausted men over ninety miles overland, by foot, on the poor roads of the seventeenth century, in September, at that high latitude, on a road that ran near the North Sea, would be a severe challenge even to the greatest logistics experts of modern times.

The main problems were food, water and shelter. It is possible that many of the Scots had embraced the old tradition of fasting for two days before a battle, to speed up their reactions: this might have been a later vestige of the medieval tradition of fasting before combat for religious reasons. These men would have been setting out for England on empty stomachs, and any edible food they had on them might already have been taken by their English captors.

It is no surprise that this grim procession soon became a death-march, even though the Scots who were forced to undertake it were not the sickest or worst injured: those had already been released. Many were new to army life, being barely-trained recent recruits, and they would be dealing with the mental trauma of what they had seen on the battlefield: men being dismembered by flying cannon-balls, stabbed with rapiers, trampled by horses; the sounds of explosions, screaming men, boys and horses: a vision of hell that would stay with them, along with the shame of defeat, further compromising their physical health.

As well as contending with hunger and thirst, many of the soldiers are known to have been inveterate pipe-smokers. If they were denied tobacco, or a means to light what tobacco they had, nicotine withdrawal-symptoms would have been fraying what fragile nerves they had left.

The Scots prisoners were likely blackened by gunpowder, particularly those who had been able to light the fuses of their muskets. They would also have been filthy and damp, their typical Scottish 'hodden grey' army-issue coats and blue bonnets stained with powder, smoke and blood, the coats turning brown in the sun, if there was any sun. Hodden grey, made by mixing wool from black and white sheep, was such a characteristic colour for both the peasantry and the armies of Scotland that it was later celebrated by Robert Burns in his poem *A Man's a Man for a' That*:

> What though on hamely fare we dine,
> Wear hodden grey, an' a that;
> Gie fools their silks, and knaves their wine;
> A Man's a Man for a' that.

We know that the prisoners included some highlanders who may have fought in tartan, but not in kilts. There were also English soldiers among them: royalists who had flocked to Charles

II's cause even though this meant fighting against their own countrymen.

When the pitiful progress reached Berwick, thirty miles south and a third of the way to Newcastle, a number of prisoners sat down and refused to move unless they were fed. Thirty of them were shot dead where they sat by Hacker's brave cavalrymen, and the death-march proceeded.

At Morpeth, nearly eighty miles from Dunbar, the prisoners were corralled in a walled garden where cabbages were grown. They descended on these vegetables like gannets and ate them raw, roots and all, despite the fact that at that time all raw food, including fruit, was thought by many to be an 'offence to the stomach'. Not surprisingly, the effect of these raw and perhaps unripe greens on their hollow bodies was to make them ill, or more ill, so much so that some thought they had poisoned themselves.

When they finally reached Newcastle, Hesilrige put them into the largest church in the city, and found that by the morning about one hundred and forty were sick. Also at Newcastle, the officers were separated out, as per Cromwell's orders: these may have numbered as many as two hundred men. The remainder now had to walk nearly twenty miles further south to Durham, where they were locked up in the cathedral. Although perhaps five thousand had left Dunbar, only three thousand were counted into the great Norman church. Allowing for the hundreds of officers, and perhaps a smaller number of sick men, who remained at Newcastle, and a number who may have been able to escape, it is still possible that well over a thousand died on the march south.

Our most important source for the death-march and the prisoners' stay in Durham is a letter written by Hesilrige to the aforementioned Council of State for Scottish and Irish Affairs, dated the second of October 1650. Hesilrige wrote his letter partly because the Council had been surprisingly prompt in coming up with instructions about what he should do with the prisoners; their orders being based on the original figures they had been given for numbers of men captured. Hesilrige had to explain to the Council that he now had far fewer Scottish prisoners at his disposal, and that some of them were still too sick to be sent anywhere.

Important as it is, Hesilrige's letter is extremely unreliable, as it was written to powerful men far away in London – men who could perhaps have engineered the author's removal from his lucrative position as governor of Newcastle, if they were unsatisfied with his work. In his letter, Hesilrige does admit that a number of the Scottish prisoners 'doubtless ran away' under cover of night, but he implies that this happened in Scotland, and not on his own turf south of the border.

Hesilrige also admits that three prisoners died at Newcastle, and that a number 'fell down in their march' and died between Newcastle and Durham; but this part of his letter leads straight into a long passage where he tries to convey the idea that what happened in Durham was not the death of many men from starvation and neglect, but a tireless losing battle fought by Hesilrige's representatives against a terrible epidemic of 'the flux'. Few of those who died, said Hesilrige, died of anything else.

According to Hesilrige, he paid out of his own pocket for plentiful food, drink and fuel for the prisoners. He had the sick taken across Palace Green from the cathedral to Durham Castle, where they were given a special diet of rich meat broths and milk boiled up with bean flour, 'the physicians holding it exceeding good for recovery of their health'. A doctor, who dressed wounds and bled his patients in line with what was considered to be best medical practice at the time, was also on hand, as were 'old women appointed to look to them in the several rooms' in the castle, which is now a college and hall of residence of Durham University.

Hesilrige's letter paints an impressive picture of the number of people employed by him to look after the prisoners. As well as the doctor and the old women who acted as nurses, there were nine men employed to 'divide' the coal that was delivered to the prisoners, as well as cooks and no less than 'forty men to cleanse and sweep them every day', the prisoners being 'sluttish', meaning dirty and untidy. According to Hesilrige, the Scots were actually 'so unruly, sluttish and nasty, that it is not to be believed; they acted rather like beasts then men'. Some of those who did not die of the flux were even murdered by their comrades, Hesilrige alleges:

for they were exceeding cruel one towards another. If a man was perceived to have any money, it was two to one but he was killed before morning, and robbed; and if any had good clothes, he that wanted [them], if he was able, would strangle him, and put on his clothes

The alleged 'sluttishness' of the Scots and their supposed murderous behaviour could be attributable to the fact that they were now leaderless men, their officers having been taken from them at Newcastle. The Scottish regiments' quartermasters, who under normal circumstances would have been responsible for the good order and healthiness of their living conditions, would have been among their lost officers, and the presence of other officers might have prevented the breakdown of discipline that led to the supposed murders.

One might be tempted to believe Hesilrige's

account of the money, time, personnel and care he expended on the Durham prisoners, if history remembered him as a civilised, compassionate, selfless and generous man. Unfortunately, that is not how history has remembered Sir Arthur Hesilrige. His one-time comrade in arms Edmund Ludlow described him as 'a man of disobliging carriage, sour and morose of temper, liable to be transported with passion, and to whom liberality seemed to be a vice'; and even his admiring biographer, Barry Denton, admitted in his 1997 book that Hesilrige's lucrative dealings as governor of Newcastle were not entirely free of greed, corruption and profiteering.

In 1650, the year of the battle of Dunbar, one John Musgrave published a paper called *A true and exact relation of the great and heavy pressures and grievances the well-affected of the northern-bordering counties lie under, by Sir Arthur Hesilrige's misgovernment;* and ten years later F. B. Gent published *The character of Sir Arthur Hazelerig, the church-thief.* Looking back on Hesilrige's highly profitable career from the perspective of 1660, Gent not only called Sir Arthur a 'church thief', but also 'a day-bed for the devil', a 'villainous rogue' and 'a dissembler and a liar'. If it is true that there really is no smoke without fire, then it would seem incautious to credit Hesilrige's assertion concerning the Scottish captives in his letter to the Council of State that 'I dare confidently say, there was never the like care taken for any such number of prisoners that ever were in England'.

It is possible that Hesilrige's letter to the Council was based on reports from his agents in Durham, including one Brewen, who is supposed to have stolen the cathedral's lectern and eagle. Hesilrige might not have visited Durham at this time, or if he did he might not have made a close inspection of the prisoners' quarters in the cathedral and castle – if he had done so, he would of course have risked catching the diseases that afflicted many of them. Although reports made to Hesilrige might have been honest about the quantities of fuel and provisions being delivered to Durham for the prisoners, they might have neglected to mention how much of this food and fuel was being diverted to their captors, and perhaps re-sold for a profit on the open market.

While it is likely that their jailers gave the Durham prisoners little more than starvation rations, they might have been very generous with their gleeful reports of how badly the war they had signed up for, now sometimes called the Third Civil War, was going for the Scots. After Dunbar, Cromwell had taken Edinburgh, and although Charles II had invaded England, his invasion failed to gain momentum, and ended in defeat at the Battle of Worcester, exactly a year after the Battle of Dunbar.

Although it is usually assumed that the missing woodwork, smashed glass and wrecked tombs at Durham, that John Barwick must have noted on his first visit as dean, were all the work of the Scottish prisoners, the chain of custody for this information is far from complete. Hesilrige's reputation as, in Gent's words, a man responsible for 'breaking up of sepulchres and searching the dormitories of the dead for hidden treasure, [and the sale of] the lead, iron bars, glass, pews, nay, pulpits' may suggest that at least some of the damage was down to Hesilrige and his agents.

If the Scots deliberately vandalised the aforementioned Neville tombs, then one can hardly blame them. They were remembering an earlier defeat of the Scots by the English at Neville's Cross near Durham in 1346. On that occasion, Ralph Neville was one of the leaders of the English force.

It is said that the Scots left the cathedral's clock untouched in 1650 because it has a thistle, a Scottish symbol, as part of its decoration; but if it was Hesilrige who ordered the removal of all the other woodwork, he may have left the clock because it was too big to remove and sell all in one piece.

Whether it was down to Hesilrige's cruel neglect, or in spite of his tender care for the Scottish prisoners, it is likely that as many as seventeen hundred of them died in Durham at this time. The rest were dispersed, perhaps over the next couple of years, to various places from which it would have been difficult for them to return to Scotland to fight for their country again.

Some were sent to King's Lynn in Norfolk to help in the giant work of draining the fens. Others were sent to fight in France and Ireland; some were encouraged to establish themselves as weavers in the north-east of England; and a number became indentured workers in the New World. The last group were in effect slaves, sold for between twenty and thirty pounds each, or about two thousand pounds in today's money. They were, however, able to buy back their freedom after seven years' servitude.

Some of the survivors of Dunbar and Durham were much better treated as indentured servants in the New World than they had been as prisoners of war in the old. Some went to work for one John Gifford in the Saugus iron-works in Lynn, Massachusetts, where Gifford built houses for them, each house to be shared between four men. The houses also had land attached, and Gifford allowed the men to split their weeks between days worked for him and time spent tending their own acres.

Other prisoners found themselves working in a sawmill on the Piscatagua river in Maine, were given twenty-five pounds each on their eventual release, and went on to become successful farmers.

Many must have died on their journeys to their new homes, especially those who were forced to make the long and perilous journey across the Atlantic. Of the one hundred and fifty who made the crossing on a small ship called the *Unity*, skippered by Augustine Walker, as many as a third may have died at sea; but others are known to have survived and prospered and founded families in America that are still going strong.

Sir Arthur Hesilrige (Patricia Brown)

IV. Jumbled Bones

In November 2013 builders working at Durham University's Palace Green library, which is just a stone's throw from the cathedral, discovered the jumbled bones of between seventeen and twenty-nine young men and boys under the floor of a disused courtyard. Scientific analysis suggested that these people had died between 1625 and 1660, and that some of them had been Scots. Nine of them had distinctive patterns of wear on their front teeth, that suggested that they had been inveterate smokers of the small clay pipes of the period. Combining the archaeological data with recorded history strongly suggested that the bones discovered belonged to a tiny fraction of the hundreds of Dunbar Martyrs who are probably still buried in the vicinity.

The jumbled state of the bones, which meant that nobody could tell exactly how many bodies they represented, suggests that they were not given a proper Christian burial, but had merely been thrown into a pit within site of the cathedral. The most horrific discovery was gnaw-marks on some of the bones: these bodies had evidently been left exposed long enough for rats and other animals to start to eat them. Could a man who took the kind of care Hesilrige claimed to have taken of his prisoners have left their dead bodies exposed to rats, denied them Christian burial, and thrown them into a pit like so much rubbish?

The courtyard under which the bones were found is now a café, a welcome refuge for visitors to the university's exhibitions, or researchers who have grown hungry or thirsty while riffling through the books held in the university's Palace Green library. The café has its own attractive courtyard, where in May 2017 a plaque was unveiled, commemorating the men and boys whose bones were found there. Also in May 2017, a new plaque was unveiled in the cathedral, replacing an earlier one that had stated that the burial-places of the Dunbar Martyrs were unknown.

Select Bibliography

Ackroyd, Peter: C*ivil War: The History of England Volume III*, Pan, 2015

Barwick, Peter: *The Life of Dr John Barwick*, Robinson, 1903

Billings, Robert William: *Architectural illustrations and description of the Cathedral Church at Durham*, T. & W. Boone, 1843

Clarendon, Edward: *Selections from Clarendon*, Oxford, 1955

Denton, Barry: *Only in Heaven*, Sheffield Academic Press, 1997

Gardiner, S.R.: *Oliver Cromwell*, Kessinger, 2004

Gaunt, Peter: *The English Civil Wars 1642-1651*, Osprey, 2003

Hopper, Andrew: *'Black Tom': Sir Thomas Fairfax and the English Revolution*, Manchester University Press, 2007

Maitland, William: *History of Edinburgh*, Hamilton, Balfour & Neil, 1753

Millward, J.S.: *Portraits and Documents,*

Seventeenth Century, Hutchinson, 1961

Parker, Geoffrey: *Global Crisis: War, Climate Change and Catastrophe in the 17th Century,* Yale, 2014

Pevsner, Nikolaus and Williamson, Angela: *The Buildings of England*: County Durham, Penguin, 1985

Reese, Peter: *Cromwell's Masterstroke: Dunbar 1650,* Pen & Sword, 2006

Reid, Stuart: *Dunbar 1650,* Osprey, 2004

Roberts, Keith: *Cromwell's War Machine: The New Model Army, 1645-1660,* Pen & Sword, 2005

Scott, Eva: *The King in Exile*, Constable, 1905

Stranks, C.J.: *This Sumptuous Church*, SPCK, 1973

Thomson, J.R.: *The Scottish Covenanters*, Bell, 1914

Weldon, J. E. C. and Wall, James: *The Story of Durham Cathedral*, Raphael Tuck (undated)

For free downloads and more from the Langley Press, please visit our website at:
http://tinyurl.com/lpdirect

Printed in Great Britain
by Amazon